You Can Beat Wall Street 'professionals'

I earn over 11% a year
So can you

Dan Keppel MBA
The Working Millionaire: $2,000,000 Tax-FREE
Wealth Reserve Self-insure Self-fund

IAN Books

An IAN Books paperback

Published by
IAN Books
41 Watchung Plaza, B242
Montclair, NJ 07042

Copyright © 2018 IAN Books

All rights reserved. No part of this book or its Interactive Internet CD can be reproduced, transmitted in any form or by any means, electronic or mechanical, including photocopying, recording, or by any information storage and retrieval system, without the written permission of the publisher.

Cover photo: Trinity students by Pete Souza

Special sales for educational use by nonprofits.
IANBooksEditor@yahoo.com

ISBN-13: 978-1986031370

ISBN-10: 1986031373

Library of Congress Control Number: 2018902554

IAN Books at Amazon.com

Wealth Without Wall Street:
Buy Direct -- Avoid the Commissions, Fees, Loads

The Insiders' Guides to Buying Discount Financial Services:
Buy Direct and Save $3,000 Every Year

Drop Your Insurance:
Buy Only What You Need

Create Financial Freedom Using Your Wealth Reserve™:
Fix your financial life

The Simple Financial Life:
How to get what you want without going into debt and living paycheck to paycheck

Build Wealth Without Extra Money or Time:
You don't need to budget or get an extra job

Tax-FREE Retirement:
Use the tax code for lifetime income free of tax

The Working Millionaire:
$2,000,000 Tax-FREE Wealth Reserve™ Self-insure Self-fund

Build Your Own $2,000,000 Tax-FREE Wealth Reserve™:
Self-insure Self-fund your lifestyle

Stop wasting $3,000 every year:
101
financial products ***NOT*** to buy and why

Long-term Care Insurance:
Is it right for you? Are there better alternatives?

Contents

Your advantage over the 'professionals'	5
1. A Tax-FREE account.	11
2. The winner's investment plan.	17
3. The miracle of compounding.	23
4. No stock picking, trading or timing.	27
5. No money manager.	33
6. Mutual funds.	39
7. Automatic Investing.	45
8. Low-cost beats high-cost.	49
9. Don't *look* twice—it's alright.	53
10. Spend wisely—it's your future.	57
Buffett won and so can you	61
The Author	65

Your advantage over the 'professionals'

"... a virtually cost-free investment in an unmanaged S&P 500 index fund – would, over time, deliver better results than those achieved by most investment professionals..." more

Warren Buffett, Chairman's Letter, p 11.
http://www.berkshirehathaway.com/2017ar/2017ar.pdf

Warren Buffett's astonishing statement comes from his recent bet. He offered $1 million to five of Wall Street's investment geniuses and he beat them with a low-cost stock market index fund.
     Hard to believe? Buffett says our advantage is no high fees, no commissions, no trading, and no market timing. Instead, compounding of a high-return diversified portfolio provides the stock market average returns of 11% over time. This is no fluke. The **average investor gives up over 7%** of their returns by using a so-called 'professional.' DALBAR found that the average investor earned only 3.79% **over time**.
     Why? It is profitable businesses that produce market returns of 11% NOT stock pickers and fast trading. Businesses are the consistent producers of value, not the smart analysts lauded for their 'flash in the pan' hits. Only Buffett has succeeded **over time**.
     He says the most important factor is compounding:

"My wealth has come from a combination of living in America, some lucky genes, and **compound interest**."

When you have stock assets, your money compounds at higher

rates when your account fees are 0.01-0.05%, not the retail rates of 1.5-3%. You don't have to settle for retail products that are structured to provide the firm **not us** with high revenues. Thus we give up over 7% of earnings when we use 'professional' managers.

The proof is Warren Buffett's strategy and this graph:

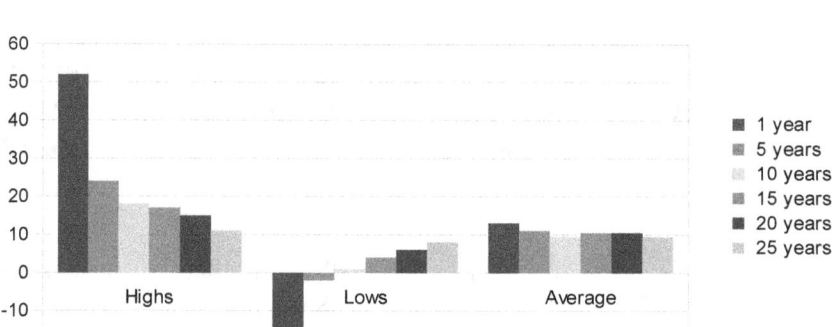

Why do otherwise smart people fall for the Wall Street myth of paying more for less? Buffett gave his opinion: they believe they are smarter than all other investors. They want instant success like some of the lucky gurus on Wall Street have found.

You are going to compound your money faster because you pay less in fees, commissions, charges and taxes. Your account will compound faster because you keep more of your money working for YOU not for a so-called 'professional.'

Wealthy people diversify their holdings so they are less likely to suffer losses. Real estate is a popular supplement asset after stocks and bonds. 77 percent of millionaire investors say they own real estate, and 35 percent say they own Real Estate Investment Trusts (REITs). This is a key finding of the Morgan Stanley Wealth Management Investor Pulse Poll. Additionally, after real estate and REITs, millionaire investors cite ownership of collectibles (34 percent), followed by precious metals (28 percent), private equity (27 percent), real assets (oil, gas, mining, 17 percent), private real estate funds (16 percent), hedge funds (16 percent), and venture capital (13 percent). Stock/bond funds have returned over 11% per year since 1976. REIT funds have returned over 10% since 1996.

Wealth people double their money every 10 years or so even if they don't have earned income. They became wealthy and stay wealthy because they use the **power of compounding**. They compound high-return assets and pay fewer fees and taxes.

Warren Buffett has shared his strategy of building assets. He is the most successful investor of our age. He buys stocks of companies we all use and holds them "forever." This strategy allows the **miracle of compounding** to work. He advises that the average investor would be better off buying a market index fund like the 500 Index (page 24) and letting compounding make them rich. Over time, the stock market earns 10-12% per year.

Buffett does *NOT* advise using Wall Street's touted top stock pickers. He knows that they are first and foremost salespeople. Their job is to bring in retail assets and sell the products that are most profitable for their firms. Wall Street firms reward their best salespeople with huge bonuses clients pay for.

Many wealthy people own their own businesses and are heavily invested in the stocks of companies they know well or do business with. Over time, their businesses paid dividends and their shares have gone up in value. Stocks of growing businesses are the *safest* investment compared with others *over time*.

Buffett cautions the average investor who is not a business professional to diversify and keep costs low. By using this strategy, the investor is "**virtually certain to get satisfactory results**."

Mr Buffett also warns investors NOT to buy and sell assets frequently. "Both individuals and institutions will constantly be urged to be active by those who profit from giving advice or effecting transactions. The resulting **frictional costs can be huge** and, for investors in aggregate, devoid of benefit. So ignore the chatter, keep your costs minimal, and invest in stocks as you would in a farm."

The wealthy know that compounding works best when they put ALL their money to work in successful businesses with few taxes or fees. They don't stop investing if their businesses have a bad day or month or even year. They realize that they can't sustain compounding with a 'buy and sell' trading method. No business person buys a business and then sells it 3 months later like money managers do. This activity creates taxes and fees. Bad for us!

Wealthy people like Mr Buffett buy a lot of stock like Coke

ONLY after they understand the company value will not be hurt by a non-critical event, like the crash of 1987. This provided Buffett's buy price with a "margin of safety," as his mentor, Benjamin Graham, called it. Buffett waits years for these non-critical events and then pounces so his investments can't lose money. And since his holding period is "forever," he does not pay capital gains taxes as it rises. He buys and holds for the **miracle of compounding**.

Another strategy of those who already have wealth is diversification. If one of their businesses slows, they still make money year over year. They would like to compound as much of their money as possible. Using 'legal' means, they avoid taxes on their accumulations and later on their withdrawals.

Wealthy business owners typically have only 21% of their net worth in their own business. They own stocks, mutual funds, land, office buildings, and other assets they believe will increase in value. Their debt is usually deductible business debt not personal debt like a mortgage on a large mansion. They are more likely to be your plumber than the image of a millionaire in the media.

Diversification is important to any person or institution with long-term wealth protection as a goal. Pension funds like the one for California workers (CalPERS) have 63% equities, 23% fixed income and 14% other assets like real estate, forests, etc. Very little is in risky investments like hedge funds or gold.

To avoid investing at the wrong time—at the top of the markets—wealthy people are **continuously invested not trading**. To avoid missing a market low point, they invest their large cash flow automatically. Compounding wealth requires consistency. Those with wealth may hold assets in cash equivalents for a time in anticipation of a large investment opportunity, but they know that **being out of the market for very long is dangerous**. The market advances in spurts and no one can forecast them in advance.

Warren Buffett's number one rule is "never lose money." To avoid making unwise investment decisions, he considers long and hard before making an investment. He follows his investment policy religiously. He consults with many people in his businesses. He never consults "high-fee managers."

So where does Buffett put his own money? Unlike most money managers, he has most of his fortune in his own business. And when he is gone, where does he direct the trustee to put all the cash? He asks that most go into the fund he used to beat the Wall

Street 'professionals': The Vanguard 500 Index fund.

Why did he specifically say Vanguard? He thinks most investors would be better off using low-cost mutual funds and NOT advisors or managers. He knows they will avoid Wall Street's fees of 1-3% and avoid unnecessary taxes. He recognizes the benefits of the **miracle of compounding**. His investment strategy is simple: let ALL your money compound in one easy to execute fund. Investors can simply set themselves up at Vanguard and let most of their wealth grow without a manager's "assistance" and fees. The 500 large businesses supply the wealth we need.

It does not take a lot of time to manage a Vanguard account. When investors don't know how to beat the market like Buffett does, it is better to let 500 successful companies do the work. Over time, Buffett believes that we will have enough assets. We won't have to worry about outliving our retirement income.

You can learn how to secure your future income too. You can start with Buffett's winning Vanguard fund. It takes only an hour per year to manage it. I think simplicity is becoming the goal of all of us. We can beat Wall Street and have enough for out future. Retirement can last for 30 years or more. In retirement, you can have the mutual fund firm deposit a fixed amount in your checking account for income while letting other assets continue to grow as before. As Warren Buffett has said:

> We continue to make more money when *snoring* than when active.
> Berkshirehathaway.com

The rich have learned that maintaining wealth is about NOT doing something stupid with their investments. Activity in investing usually is the result of fear or greed. Activity usually costs more than the gains. They only act after considerable discussion with the folks they trust and Wall Street is usually not on their list.

They have learned that building a lifetime business takes patience and time. They have learned to live below their means. They have patiently invested in their own businesses and the businesses owned by the mutual funds they bought long ago. Mr Crawley, a parking lot attendant did it: http://www.youtube.com/watch?v=XD0svDGyLWU When you invest, you need to keep it simple as I and most of my former clients have done for years.

Buffett's advice is working. The only large mutual fund

complex that attracted money last year was Vanguard. Investors are moving from high-cost managed accounts to the largest mutual fund provider—Vanguard. With costs under 0.2% compared with giving up 63% of earnings to managers, people are realizing that "cost matters," to quote John Bogle.

Buffett suggests that we must recognize that the number one factor in maintaining wealth is **maximizing the miracle of compounding**. I learned this from my boss in the 80's. He told me that we must allow our money to grow with low fees and taxes. Fees are easily controlled. Vanguard provides both low-cost index funds AND low-cost managed funds. Taxes destroy compounding. I show you how to avoid taxes using a special account.

Buffett also points out that Vanguard has licensed financial experts to help. They are salaried, not commissioned. This provides those who need some assurance with less biased confirmation of their own investment choices. So, even the younger or up-and-coming millionaires can easily get help when they need it without a formal and costly Wall Street relationship. The larger fund firms can provide most of the services that are provided by any full-service Wall Street brokerage firm. Discount brokers have many of the same services for less if the wealthy wish to hold securities at no cost and no taxes until they sell.

You can use Buffett's time-tested strategy to maintain Wealth without Wall Street. When you have assets, you know how much you can spend each year. Moving to a Simple Financial Life will allow you the freedom to enjoy your life. It also will reduce your fees, commissions, and charges providing more money. You lower taxes by not trading. Following Buffett's strategy provides peace of mind. You know your assets are growing. Buffett's advice:

"... the 'know-nothing' investor who both diversifies and keeps his costs minimal is virtually certain to get satisfactory results."

http://www.berkshirehathaway.com/2013ar/2013ar.pdf

A Tax-FREE account

One of the strategies of the wealthy is to avoid taxes on their accumulations. Consider these examples: When you have money, you can use all the legal means to avoid taxes. For instance, Warren Buffett, with $80 billions, pays only 17% **total** tax: http://www.youtube.com/watch?v=Cu5B-2LoC4s; Mitt Romney only **14%**; John Kerry only **13%** and Apple just **9.8%**. Buffett admits that his staff pays **32.9%**—DOUBLE! Most of the top 1% pay far less than the average citizen of this country in terms of disposable income.

If the average family earns $85,000, they pay about 14% federal, 13% SS/Med/UC/Health, 10% state/local, 4% sales/excise, or over 30% total taxes. As Buffett said, "I pay 17.7% total tax. My office staff pays 32.9%." Of course this does not include pension and other insurance costs most Americans also pay.

This is why the wealthy avoid taxes with their own businesses and various tax-advantaged vehicles. In order to become and stay wealthy, people need to have money to invest. The average family has little extra money to build wealth let alone have enough for retirement. They need tax-FREE compounding.

Corporations and businesses can control taxes as an expense by using all the legal means they can afford to pay for. Apple was hauled before Congress in 2013 to explain how it avoids the rate the IRS code mandates—35%. It has subsidiaries around the world so its lawyers and accountants can avoid taxes.

Nearly every major firm has its share of tax tricks up its sleeve. Apple accomplishes this feat with a two-pronged tax strategy. For domestic sales, the company pays profits as a royalty on a subsidiary it owns in Ireland, which are then routed to a tax haven. For overseas sales, the company uses a second Irish sub, routes the profits through The Netherlands to avoid European taxes, and then sends its profits to its tax haven via the first Irish sub. This sub is called a **"disregarded entity"**—an affiliate not subject to U.S. income tax. (This strategy is called the "Double Irish with a Dutch Sandwich," this report says.)

Some smart working folks have found a way to buyout their boss's firm. Some wealthy people have followed this path. They are <u>The Working Millionaires</u>. They have learned that building wealth takes time. Most of my former clients own a business or two. It may take a lifetime to create a sustainable income source and possible retirement treasury. They eventually learn to utilize the system and save on taxes and fees. That is really the only way most Americans can become wealthy.

Some clients have built their wealth by using some of their salary, partnerships or other relationships with others. They invested their money, usually in opportunities that were not open to the public. Others just worked hard and invested. They accumulated $1 million or so over time using a mutual fund or broker. They double it every 10 years or so.

If you do not have a business to help avoid taxes, one of the best ways for a salaried person to accumulate your first $1 million is to use a tax-FREE account called a Roth IRA. You can avoid all taxes on your investments as they grow and on withdrawals. This account is offered by all the large mutual fund companies like Vanguard, Fidelity, TIAA, and Schwab.

You can then buy mutual funds or securities that can earn 10% to 12% a year, year after year. You could probably put other investments in this account, but we need to understand the reward and risk characteristics of them first. I will explain why stocks are the most secure investment for long-term wealth-building below.

For now, you need to consider the fact that if we want to have a balance of $1 million; we would have to wait 100 years for a minimum contribution of say $250 a month to grow in a CD at 2%. Investing in stocks provides almost the reverse risk profile. Historically, the value of a stock market index—a bunch of stocks—has varied greatly in any one year. However, over time, the value has ALWAYS increased. This is the reason wealthy people have most of their money in the stocks of growing companies.

Remember, we are looking for an investment that compounds our money at 10-12% year after year. The reward and risk profile of owning a bunch of stocks is like owning a business—in any one year, we might have a loss or we might profit. But over time we have more profits than losses and thus succeed.

After you are wealthy, you can leave some of your money in CDs and US treasuries for liquidity purposes. Bank savings are a great place to park our money for a year in case you need it to take advantage of an investment opportunity.

However, bank savings are not really an investment. People who put all their money in the bank because they think it is "safe" are not thinking about the long-term. They are actually losing money. Inflation is eating away at the value of their savings.

Inflation is historically about 3%. If we earn 3% or less on our money, we are losing purchasing power. Wealthy people make sure part of their portfolio is liquid. They don't want to have to sell one of their businesses or one of their long-held securities in order to raise cash for any reason. This activity creates taxes.

There are few investments that we can buy that have the same long-term annual returns of stocks of growing companies. The graph below presents the relative growth of different types of investments and inflation.

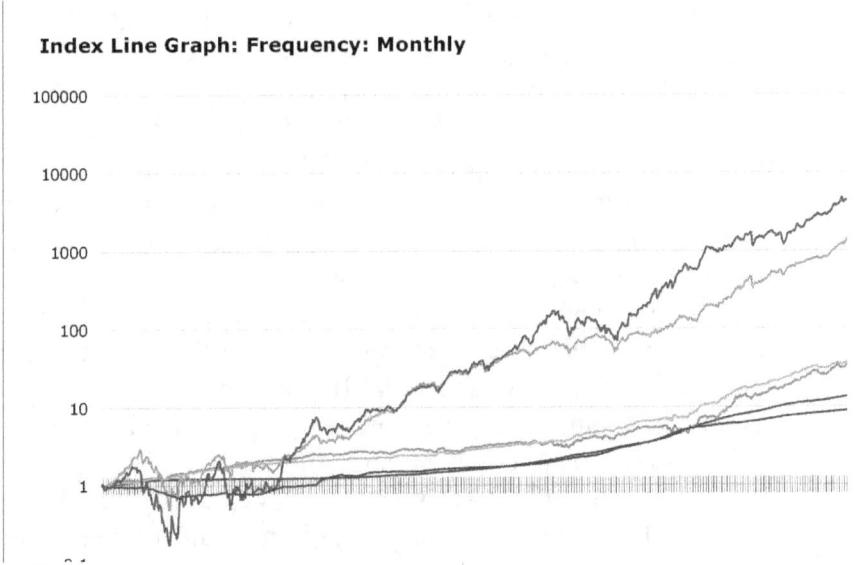

Top line—Small Cap Stocks
2nd line—Large Cap Stocks (S&P 500)
3rd line—US Long-term Corporate Bonds
4th line—Intermediate-term Government Bonds
5th line—US 30 day Government T-bills
6th line—US inflation

Courtesy: Dr. Campbell R. Harvey http://www.duke.edu/~charvey/

Over long-periods of time, government bonds grow at a rate a little above the rate of inflation. Large company stocks like GE and P&G grow at a higher rate and thus accumulate larger values in our account. Smaller companies grow much faster and make our account even larger over time. However, as the graph shows, the index line can be very jagged on a monthly and even yearly basis. Values do go up over time.

This graph makes it pretty clear that in order to accumulate $1,000,000 from monthly contributions, we must buy and hold the securities of growing companies worldwide AND pay **zero** tax on the growth to maximize compounding. We can see clearly that investing in growing company stocks is more likely to get us to our goal in our lifetime than investing in government bonds or a bank savings account.

This graph shows the accumulation over time without paying taxes each year on our earnings or annual fees to an advisor or broker. It does show that over most periods greater than 10 years, our account value grows more with stocks.

Some wealthy people also invest in gold, real estate, and alternative investment schemes. But these investments do NOT usually represent a large portion of their portfolio. These investments do not come without significant costs and significant risk. They do NOT show the same consistent long-term growth pattern that global growing companies do.

As your investments grow—especially mutual funds that pay dividends and gains each year—you will not have to pay tax on them because of your special IRS-approved account. Most regular IRAs and pension accounts are tax-DEFERRED not tax-FREE. Taxes have to be paid sometime.

Your Roth IRA allows you to leverage tax-FREE accumulations over time against an immediate tax deduction as with a regular IRA or 401k pension. The benefits can be enormous. For instance, if you make contributions of $250 a month, $3,000 a year to your low-cost stock mutual funds, you could spend $30,000 tax-FREE for every $3,000 you deposited!

You invest $99,000 and grow your account to $1 million in about 33 years, $2 million in 40 and $3 million in 42. You pay no tax on the reinvested dividends and gains as your account grows and NO tax when you spend your accumulations. And, you can avoid Wall Street's commissions, fees, loads, and charges. Some savvy investors have already decided to go this route. I would be surprised if more didn't follow.

If an investment requires taxes and fees to be paid each year, this cancels some of the compounding effect on the total accumulation over time. Since we wish to reach our first $1 million as soon as possible, we must use a tax-FREE account to hold our investments. Without this account, we may reduce our total accumulation by half because we lose the compounding effect. The chart below gives us an idea of what can happen over time.

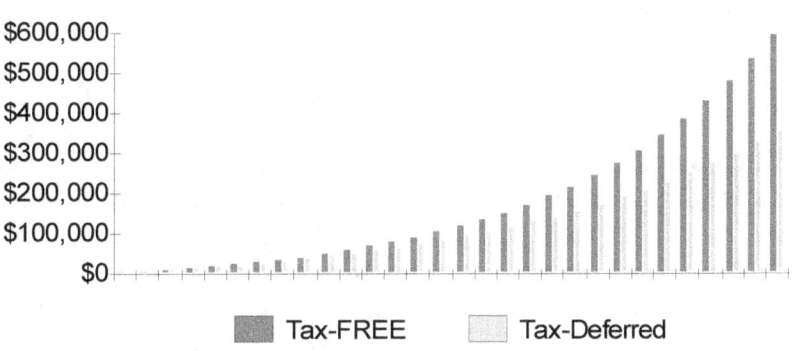

The American tax system taxes <u>earned</u> income at higher rates than <u>investment</u> income. Thus we must pay federal and state income taxes, excise taxes, Social Security and Medicare taxes, perhaps unemployment and disability income taxes as well as sales tax on most goods.

Traditional pensions, 401k and IRAs just delay taxes—taxes must be paid later as the money comes out of the account AND at higher **earned income** tax rates. Thus even when our investment money is growing it is converted to earned income money for tax purposes. Unlike Mr Buffett, we would NEVER get to pay the wealthy people rate of 15% without a tax-FREE trust.

Luckily, there is now a solution for you to match the tax advantage of the wealthy. In fact, only you can use it. Warren Buffett and Mitt Romney earn too much to use this trust.

Senator Roth introduced the Roth IRA in 1997. This tax-FREE account provides the protection you need to allow your contributions to compound without taxation every year AND later when you take them out, you **never have to pay taxes** on the earnings, dividends and interest you earn on your money. You don't even pay the tax-advantaged rate of the wealthy!

Ben Franklin was wrong! Only death is certain, not taxes. The only thing you give up with this account is an immediate tax deduction. This is a better deal than most wealthy people have. Tax-FREE accumulation and tax-FREE income after age 59.5 is a huge bonus. It is like receiving $250,000 FREE on your $1 million account. Also, because you already paid tax on the contributions, you pay no tax when you borrow contributions during your lifetimes. This can make a big impact on your borrowing costs when you take money out to buy an appliance, a car, a down payment or living expenses.

Using this account, our total contributions of $99,000 over time grow to over $1,000,000 and we don't have to pay any federal or state income tax on the earnings. Since we pay no tax, Uncle Sam is really helping us out in meeting our goal. All we have to do is use this special IRS tax haven and keep making contributions.

This special account is the IRS §408 trust. We have to follow the rules to gain this amazing tax advantage but the Roth IRA rules are pretty simple—taxed money goes in and tax-FREE earnings come out after age 59 ½. You can take your contributions out anytime after 5 years.

Why is this account special? Every other type of investment account requires that taxes be paid now or later. Mutual funds declare gains each year just like a bank CD and we need to pay tax. Our retirement accounts and annuities are tax-deferred. We pay tax when we take money out. Even life insurance with cash value requires taxes to be paid unless it is a death benefit to heirs. Even assets like individual stocks or ETFs or our own company equity held for long term gains will require taxes eventually when sold.

Contributions are limited to $5,500 (2013), but may rise in future years. http://www.irs.gov/publications/p590/ch02.html There are income limits but most people don't hit the earnings limit of $128,000 (2013) until later. If we are married, the limit is $188,000 (2013).

We may also invest in our employer's Roth 401k if it is offered. The contributions grow tax FREE forever. We can contribute up to $17,500 (2013). We will have tax-FREE income from the account later.

We can make contributions to our Roth 401k only if our employer offers it in the retirement plan. Many young people prefer to be taxed at the beginning of their careers since their salaries do not draw high tax rates yet. The contribution limit may be raised in the future.

There are no limits on an employee's income in determining if he or she can make designated Roth 401(k) contributions. If we decide to invest $10,000 a year for 35 years in a low-cost stock fund inside our employer's Roth 401k plan, we could accumulate $2 million with NO income taxation to pay on the earnings. The tax savings might be worth an extra 30% since our federal and state tax payments are avoided.

The catch: If we take the *earnings* out before age 59.5, we must pay income tax, unless we use $10,000 for our first home, are disabled, or die. The account must be open at least 5 years to take money out. However, if we take out *contributions*, we pay no tax. If we pay our 'loan' back to our own account, we can still reach our goal. The hard part is leaving our money alone to grow tax-FREE.

Let's say we need $20,000 to buy a new used car. As we can see from the chart on page 22, taking $20,000 from an account worth $250,000 is very different from taking $20,000 from one worth only $50,000. Both are contributions and are not taxable but borrowing 40% of the account this early stunts its growth.

The payoff: The chart below shows how your money can grow tax-FREE and fee-FREE. When you and your spouse contribute $250 a month to your Roth IRAs, your family can accumulate enough for retirement and serious medical needs. You might even have enough for an inheritance. This shows the power of compounding without Wall Street. You clean up on Wall Street!

Monthly Accumulation at 12% per year										
	5	10	15	20	25	30	35	40	45	50
$100	$8,167	$23,004	$49,958	$98,925	$187,884	$349,496	$643,095	$1,176,477	$2,145,469	$3,905,834
$200	$16,334	$46,008	$99,916	$197,850	$375,768	$698,992	$1,286,190	$2,352,954	$4,290,938	$7,811,668
$300	$24,501	$69,012	$149,874	$296,775	$563,652	$1,048,488	$1,929,285	$3,529,431	$6,436,408	$11,717,502
$500	$40,835	$115,020	$249,790	$494,625	$939,420	$1,747,480	$3,215,475	$5,882,385	$10,727,346	$19,529,169

The Roth IRA Rules

Contributions:

$5,500 ($6,500 over age 50) each year
Income under $135,000 (2018) single
$195,000 married (2018)

Distributions:

Tax-FREE for contributions.
And Tax-FREE for earnings if
Over age 59 1/2,
Account open 5 years,
Taxable earnings unless
Disabled,
First home ($10,000),
Death

Bonus:

Account can grow tax-FREE for life
Minimum distribution rules don't apply
Heirs don't pay income tax
Account has no maximum

Check with your tax preparer
https://www.irs.gov/pub/irs-pdf/p590a.pdf

The winner's investment plan

Our working millionaire would find a way to save the $20,000 separately or keep driving the old car. The power of compounding is too valuable to lose by raiding the account too early. One story about billionaire Buffett will illustrate the habits of the wealthy. Mr Buffett is said to have driven (still no chauffeur) his VW Beetle long after he became a multimillionaire. Buffett did not like to lose money and a new car loses 40% of its value quickly. He thought that the $35,000 a new car cost, invested at 10-12% is worth about $80,000 in 10 years. So he kept driving his old VW.

    Most clients are not that thrifty. However, if your income has not yet exceeded the Roth IRA limit, you can use your tax-FREE contributions to buy without paying loan interest. You pay cash for a used car to avoid new car depreciation and new appliances, vacations, and other necessities. AFTER you have let your contributions compound, you can "borrow" them interest FREE. When **both** family wage earners contribute to their Roth IRAs, you can easily reach a quarter of a million dollars in 15 years. That means $90,000 are contributions and then some of them can be used to pay cash instead of buying on credit.

    Our clients pay cash. They never PAY interest. Paying interest on non-income producing assets is the reverse of compounding. Someone else is becoming wealthy from them. The wealthy always EARN interest. They use this calculator moneychimp.com/calculator/compound_interest_calculator.htm to determine what the real cost of buying something on credit will be just as Buffett did. Why give up $80,000 when we can drive the old car a little longer? Buffett could have bought 100 new cars and it wouldn't have changed his wealth or lifestyle, but he didn't. His habit is to live frugally. He still lives in his first $31,500 home.

    You can use this account (its contributions) to cover your liability insurance deductibles if needed. Over time, you can save thousands of dollars by using the highest deductibles on your car, home and health insurance. **Self-insurance** is also the way to avoid any changes in your policy costs. Insurers are less likely to drop you if you don't make claims for small amounts. If you take care of your out-of-pocket medical expenses, you may find a low-cost comprehensive policy if you need to buy health coverage.

The rules for the use of your Roth IRA account are manageable by yourself. You don't need an advisor. They are found at irs.gov/retirement/article/0,,id=137307,00.html. Your account trustee can answer most questions. You don't need to pay an attorney. All of the large low-cost mutual funds firms are trustees. I will discuss the best firms available below.

You can start this account with any of the firms with no upfront charges. Most do charge an annual fee for the initial investments. Charges are reduced later. We will consider the specific investment options later. We will use low-cost firms because you will keep more of your own money. You don't need to pay Wall Street to maintain this account.

It is important to pick a trustee with the least costs since over time the annual costs can really destroy your accumulations. For instance, if you use a brokerage firm like ours as trustee, you might have to pay 2-3% or more each year on the balance. The difference is huge. If both spouses have a low-cost account with contributions of $250 a month for 37 years, they could accumulate $3,000,000. If they use a high-cost broker/advisor, both accounts may hit only $1,300,000. Depending on earnings of 8-10% and total costs of 2% per year, you could really hurt yourself. You need to watch the costs. Advisors do NOT beat the markets over the long term. Just stick with your investment plan.

You can open your account at any age as long as you have *earned* income. Stock dividends or interest do not count. I can't use a Roth unfortunately. Any job will do. You don't even need a job requiring a W-2 to prove it. A part-time, weekend or night job will do. Any cash-only work will qualify—even for a child. I think accountants recommend that receipts and records be maintained. You could even work for yourself in a home-office business.

Nontaxable distributions from a Roth IRA won't affect your eligibility for student aid either. Later, in retirement, this money won't affect your social security benefits as of the rules today.

You can make contributions to both your individual Roth IRA and your Roth account at work (401k, 403b, 457b). The limits change each year, so check Pub 590a: http://www.irs.gov/pub/irs-pdf/p590a.pdf. The 2018 limits are $5,500 ($1,000) and $18,500 ($5,500) respectively. (We can make catch-up contributions to both.) Wage limit for singles is $135,000; $195,000 married.

Higher income earners can build a non-deductible IRA and then convert it to a Roth IRA, paying taxes on the converted amount in stages. This gives higher tax-FREE accumulations later on. If you convert right away, there may be no gain and thus you never have to pay tax on this money ever again. Typically, all tax-deferred retirement plans are taxable. This one is FREE.

Avoiding taxes on your annual gains supercharges your accumulations. This special account is the IRS §408 trust or Roth IRA. You have to follow the rules of a Roth IRA to gain this amazing tax advantage. The rules are pretty simple: pay smaller taxes on contributions now in exchange for NO tax on huge gains later. You can 'borrow' the contributions to avoid paying interest to banks for our major purchases. You earn interest, you don't pay interest. This is the perfect tax shelter for any working person. And you can beat Wall Street because it is free to set up and run each year. In the future, we can spend tax-FREE $30,000 for every $3,000 we invest today.

See the client account below: $1 million in 32 years. He never let Wall Street 'professionals' touch his money. It is important to just stick with the winner's plan. Wall Street 'professionals' do NOT give refunds if they fail you.

The *Miracle of Compounding* does the work, not stock pickers.

Actual client, Tom's account, investing $3,000 per year, 1962-2003

24%	3,720
16%	7,795
12%	12,091
-10%	13,582
24%	20,561
11%	26,153
-8%	26,821
4%	31,013
14%	38,775
19%	49,713
-14%	45,333
-26%	35,766
37%	53,110
24%	69,576
-8%	66,770
6%	73,956
18%	90,809
32%	123,827
-5%	120,486
22%	150,653
21%	185,920
6%	200,255
32%	268,297
19%	322,843
5%	342,135
17%	403,808
32%	536,987
-3%	523,787
31%	690,091
8%	748,538
10%	826,692
2%	846,286
38%	1,172,015
23%	1,445,268
33%	1,926,197
28%	2,469,372
21%	2,991,570
-9%	2,725,059
-12%	2,403,420
-22%	1,874,601
29%	2,412,905

The miracle of compounding

Compounding high earnings is your *best* strategy. The wealthy get richer just by leaving their money invested. They don't work more hours or take more risks. The famous 1% at the top of society takes down 23.5% of all income (up from 8.9% 30 years ago). Most of the increase is from compound earnings. They don't work any harder than you do—their money does.

Because of compounding, many millionaires have said, "the first million was the hardest." If a working business person has accumulated $250,000, it takes her or him 20 years to grow it to $1,000,000 using tax-advantaged investments. However, it only takes 7-9 years to double their money. Investors in stock funds, earning 10-12% on average, can double it again to $2 million in less than 10 years without adding new money. Their tax-advantaged accounts make it easier to reach their goal. It is compounding that makes it happen—not Wall Street brokers.

Compounding of high earnings means that we make money on our last period's accumulations. The progression looks like the client's account values on the previous page. Notice that our balance can double in a couple of good years. This happens because we are not just adding $3,000 per year, but adding up to 38% of the previous year's accumulation to our balance. We are making money on top of our money with no extra effort on our part. During this 40 year period, this client 'lost' money some years. In fact, they 'lost' 14% and then 26% back to back, but then made 37% and 24%. They didn't *lose* since they did not sell shares

Wealthy people don't panic. They have learned that long-term compounding is the only way they can build wealth. There are no successful get rich quick schemes. To reach their goal, they know there will be setbacks. No business grows steadily upward all the time. See Apple. They have seen the losses before and they don't sell their assets in a panic.

We will buy assets that "grow by themselves." We will have security because our ***purchasing power*** will grow over time. If we doubt that the wealthy invest in the stock market for security, take a look at the long-term returns for various Vanguard mutual funds where they put their money. These funds have provided investors with $1,000,000 or more for their retirement. During the recent recessions, Vanguard had inflows not outflows.

The wealthy earn 10% to 12% on their money. Some buy all ten Vanguard funds and receive 11% total return with less risk than owning just one fund. When one fund is down, others are up.

2017 Total Return	Fund	Long-term Return	Longevity
21.7%	500 Index	11.1%*	since 1976
3.2%	Energy	10.7%	since 1984
17.9%	Extended Market	10.9%	since 1987
19.6%	Health	16.5%	since 1984
42.9%	International Growth	10.8%	since 1981
29.5%	PRIMECAP	13.9%	since 1984
16.1%	Small Cap Index	10.7%	since 1960
10.2%	Wellesley Income	9.9%	since 1970
19.1%	Windsor	11.5%	since 1958
16.8%	Windsor II	10.8%	since 1985
19.7%	Average	11.7%	

*Average Annual Returns as of 12/31/17.

This kind of security comes from our regular contributions ... and *patience*. The miracle of compounding works its magic on our Roth IRA account when we give it TIME. The wealthy give their money time to compound. They don't take it out. They try not to pay tax every year on the gains. They maintain their contribution schedule because each $100 added is worth $10,000 to them later. They use the compound interest calculator so they know the future value: moneychimp.com/calculator/compound_interest_calculator.htm.

Compounding of high earnings requires patience but has a big bang. Most people who become wealthy have to wait for years of slow growth in their account. At the beginning of the accumulation, especially if we have a loss or two, we are very tempted to get discouraged and quit making contributions. The account just doesn't seem to adding up to an inspiring total.

It took client Tom 21 years to get to $150,000. Then it only took 14 years to get to a $1,172,015. After only 4 years, it became $3,000,000. Shortly thereafter he 'lost' over a million dollars!

This client stuck with it and was successful in reaching the goal but there are many who do not. Most people who are not wealthy already, have a hard time believing it can happen with their patience. They just don't have the experience of how compounding works to keep faith in its outcome eventually.

If you already have an Roth IRA account with significant values, you can use it to do your gift and estate planning. You don't have to take the money out beginning at age 70½, unlike the regular IRA or pension. You can let it grow. You can name your family members as beneficiaries which will be effective for both property law and income tax purposes. Obviously, as beneficiary, your grandchild could just liquidate the account and thus lose the value for their "*Gift of a Lifetime*." Wealthy people use a knowledgable attorney to make sure their wealth passes to those who make the most of it.

Once an account becomes sizable, we don't need to add contributions to it. Usually, by the time we stop regular employment, we aren't making contributions. This account cannot accept contributions unless they are the result of earned income. Some wealthy people continue to work after age 65 because they love what they do and want to continue. Obviously, they don't need to work. The **miracle of compounding** continues to work.

One of the best examples of the potential of growth by compounding is seen in the accumulation of investor Anne Scheiber. With below average wages, this woman invested in quality companies which paid dividends and gains. She did not sell so she didn't have taxes on gains. She reinvested her dividends and gains and at her death gave $22 million to Yeshiva University for a scholarship designed to help support deserving women.

The Miracle of Compounding doubles our money in 7-9 years when we put it to work in high earning company stocks. We don't have to do anything except let it work. Warren Buffett reminds us that this is the key to investing success by proving again that Wall Street 'professionals' are NOT right for us.

The annual returns of growing companies

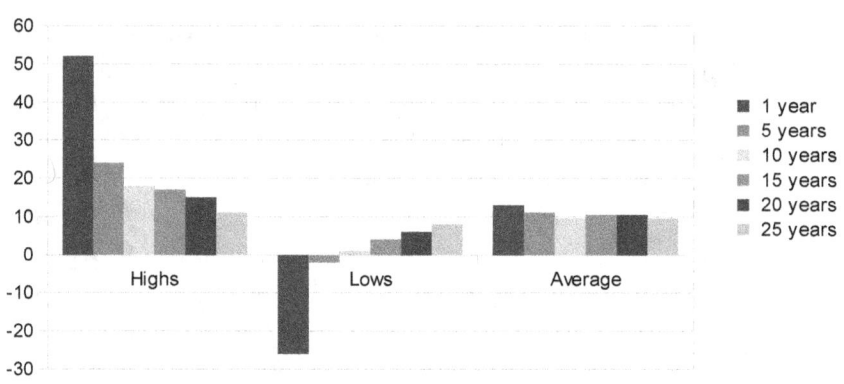

No stock picking, trading or timing

This investing method is usually overlooked by those who need to understand it the most. To grow wealth, we have to maintain consistent contributions to it. It seems self evident but I guess if we don't learn to put money away early in our lives, we are not in the habit. And there is always an emergency for our cash.

When we develop the habit of investing, we take our emotions out of the process. If we do not watch the stock market or our account balance regularly, we will be less likely to panic. If we don't have to send the contribution each month, we don't think about how our account is doing. It will grow as on page 30.

Most people want to watch their money. They have no experience of building a business by putting their own money into it and sometimes seeing the VALUE go down. But the business does not fail. It continues. We, as a silent partner must learn to live with this rise and fall. We have to believe that not all global businesses will fail. They will continue to grow. We need to think of this account as our stake in growing businesses.

One way we can help change our thinking is to put the account out of our immediate concern by making the contributions automatic. Like the Social Security contributions we make every payday, the contributions come out of our pay automatically. This can happen easily with a Roth 401k since our Plan administrator will deduct the amount we specify at Plan enrollment. In the same manner, we can have the Roth IRA trustee debit our checking account automatically every period.

As one client told me, "I never see the deduction, so I never miss it." Of course this client has already identified the $250 he has committed to his $1,000,000 future. He says that he would just waste the $250 anyway. He had been doing that for years because he never took the trouble to set his goals for short-term and long-term timelines. He took my advice and went through his spending on financial services. He used our *Guides* to find the $250 a month he was wasting on products and services he would never use or need. In my book amazon.com/Insiders-Guides-Discount-

Financial-Services/ you will find **"tricks of the trade"** that we insiders use to buy directly from quality manufacturers.

Many people have trouble keeping up the habit of investing every month. Some emergency always interupts this process. The delay in the periodic contributions causes the compounding effect to be reduced. The interruption is like starting the investment process late. This chart shows us what starting early or not putting off the investments can do. Over time, the delay compounds the lack of accumulation. Starting 5 years later means ending up with HALF the amount we were shooting for. It is hard to believe that missing that $250 a month for 5 years or $15,000 can reduce our total from $600,000 to $300,000. It's easy to say **I will start later**.

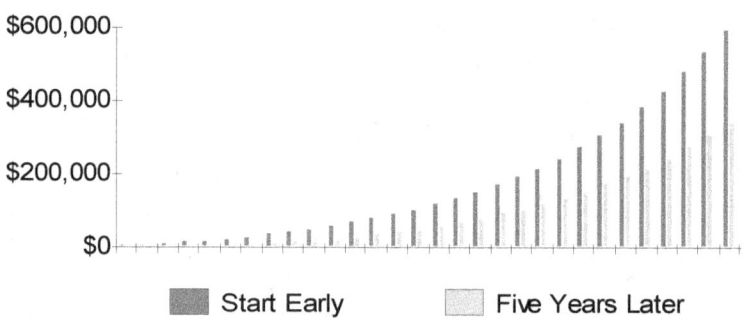

This is why our contributions to the account should not pass through our hands. We should have the money taken directly from our bank account by the trustee. Contributions are after-tax so you can take them back, if necessary, with no tax payable. Nontaxable distributions from a Roth IRA won't affect your eligibility for student aid either. Later, in retirement, this money won't affect your Social Security benefits as of the rules today.

The second reason why this technique for developing wealth works is that when contributions are automatic, we do not have the temptation to try to time the market. Many people want to know the secret to timing the market so that they can invest right at the bottom of market cycles and sell at the peak of the market.

Unfortunately, it is a myth that we can do this over time. Again, this is our misconception of how building wealth works.

Yes there are Wall Street gurus who have records. However, they are the exception and we don't know which to pick NOW. We are trying to build wealth over time. We want to end up with $1,000,000 tax-FREE. We are silent partners in building businesses that produce dividends and gains over time. We are not placing our contributions on the red or black at the casino.

Our account grows with steady contributions because in the month we buy $250 of company stocks in a mutual fund, we receive less shares when the price is high and more shares when the price is low. Studies have shown that this is better than investing our $3,000 all at once. It is not possible to know when the shares we buy will be at their lowest cost in the year going forward. Again, over time, we will own more shares at the least cost because we are buying more when the price is low.

This can be illustrated by considering how hard it is to find the lowest price at any given time in the market. There were ONLY 40 days from 1950 to 2007 that produced 70% of all the S&P 500 index's total returns. That is 40 out of 14,528. We can't possibly know when to buy into the businesses represented in the mutual fund we are using. We will lose money if we try to become traders who time the market. John Bogle's analysis in *Don't Count on It*, p 169 is correct. I have tried various strategies and failed.

The key to building wealth is steady growth. We have seen that over time, stocks of growing companies have the most consistent record of providing 10-12% annual returns. We just don't know **which** companies and **which** time to invest are best. Luckily, we don't have to know. We need to understand the bigger picture on page 30.

The bigger picture is that we want our account accumulation to grow exponentially. We want to take advantage of the miracle of compounding. Since we don't have a million dollars, we are going to have to be patient to acquire it. We want every dollar we invest to count. We have $250 a month to invest so we have to rely on consistent buying of shares to reach our goal.

Accumulations double in value every 7-9 years if they are concentrated in the top two graph lines below. Of course the stock market doesn't move up at 10-12% EACH year. However, our wealth account will double and double and double so that by age 65, we could have over $1 million. Notice how the account values in the chart on page 22 for our client Tom move from $1 million to

$2 million in 8 years, even with 3 years of losses. Of course, a million dollars will be worth less in the future because of inflation. But we will certainly appreciate our account values later no matter what our contributions are now. Consistency builds wealth.

Cumulative Wealth

Top line—Small Cap Stocks
2nd line—Large Cap Stocks (S&P 500)
3rd line—US Long-term Corporate Bonds
4th line—Intermediate-term Government Bonds
5th line—US 30 day Government T-bills
6th line—US inflation

Courtesy: Dr. Campbell R. Harvey http://www.duke.edu/~charvey/

And the bonus of this geometric account growth is that it does not quit even after we stop adding our monthly contributions. Once the account has reached a certain mass, let's say after 20 years of $250 contributions or $160,000, it will keep compounding. On page 32 we show you how this worked for contributions of $2,000 to a virtual account invested in the U.S. stock market (500 Index) over time.

We can see, in the chart "Cumulative Wealth" above, that over time wealth accumulates at different rates depending on the type of assets we buy. For anyone who invested in smaller companies over any given 15 year period, the benefits were outstanding. For each $1,000 invested in 1940, $3,000,000 was the total return by the 1990's. Investing more cautiously in the large companies of the S&P 500, for instance, our single $1,000 would have grown to almost a $1,000,00 by 2000. Yes, the lines are not perfectly straight, but growing $250 a month to $1 million is definitely worth the ups and downs. Inflation is designated by the bottom line here. Putting all our money in "safe" investments would accumulate at a rate represented by a line near that bottom line.

Of course, these different rates of wealth accumulation assume two important factors—NO taxes and NO costs. We have eliminated the first killer of wealth—TAXES—by using a tax-FREE trust account. Costs of the investment type we use can also kill your total accumulations. My whole industry is built on the extraction of these costs from the accounts of investors like you. You must use low-cost stock funds to obtain high returns.

The main reason people hire Wall Street firms is to "watch" their money. Our clients are paying us millions of dollars for peace of mind. They think that we can see the future and stop any loss in their accounts. Unfortunately, this is just an illusion we maintain.

You can avoid paying us up to 63% of your eventual total wealth by learning to stick with the program. You can just put your contributions on automatic. Your trustee will debit your checking account every month. You can call them when the market scares you. You have a higher probability of meeting your goals over time by not watching. I look at the graph on page 30 when I hear 'crash.' After going through a couple of crises, we forget we are investing in our future and thus we actually create one.

The Miracle of Compounding only happens with consistent contributions to a market index fund. Warren Buffett has never been a stock "trader." He buys and **holds** businesses "forever." Even a great investor like Buffett has trouble finding profitable stocks to buy. That is why John Bogle, founder, Vanguard mutual funds says "Don't look for the needle in the haystack. Just buy the haystack."

$2,000 Annual Stock Market Investment 1950- '70- '80- '90- 2013

Year	Returns	Balance	Balance	Balance	Balance
		$2,000			
1950	31%	$2,620			
1951	24%	$5,729			
1952	18%	$9,120			
1953	-1%	$11,009			
1954	52%	$19,773			
1955	31%	$28,523			
1956	5%	$32,049			
1957	-11%	$30,304			
1958	43%	$46,194			
1959	12%	$53,978			
1960	1%	$56,538			
1961	26%	$73,757			
1962	-8%	$69,697			
1963	24%	$88,904			
1964	16%	$105,449			
1965	12%	$120,342			
1966	-10%	$110,108			
1967	24%	$139,014			
1968	11%	$156,526			
1969	-8%	$145,844	2,000		
1970	4%	$153,757	2,080		
1971	14%	$177,563	4,651		
1972	19%	$213,681	7,915		
1973	-14%	$185,485	8,527		
1974	-26%	$138,739	7,790		
1975	37%	$192,813	13,412		
1976	24%	$241,568	19,111		
1977	-8%	$224,082	19,422		
1978	6%	$239,647	22,707		
1979	18%	$285,144	29,155	2,000	
1980	32%	$379,030	41,124	2,640	
1981	-5%	$361,978	40,968	4,408	
1982	22%	$444,053	52,421	7,818	
1983	21%	$539,724	65,850	11,879	
1984	6%	$574,228	71,921	14,712	
1985	32%	$760,621	97,575	22,060	
1986	19%	$907,519	118,494	28,632	
1987	5%	$954,995	126,519	32,163	
1988	17%	$1,119,684	150,367	39,971	
1989	32%	$1,480,623	201,125	55,402	2,000
1990	-3%	$1,438,144	197,031	55,680	1,940
1991	31%	$1,886,589	260,731	75,560	5,161
1992	8%	$2,039,676	283,749	83,765	7,734
1993	10%	$2,245,843	314,324	94,342	10,708
1994	2%	$2,292,800	322,651	98,268	12,962
1995	38%	$3,166,824	448,018	138,370	20,647
1996	23%	$3,897,654	553,522	172,656	27,856
1997	33%	$5,186,540	738,844	232,292	39,709
1998	28%	$6,641,331	948,281	299,894	53,387
1999	21%	$8,038,430	1,149,839	365,291	67,019
2000	-9%	$7,316,791	1,048,174	334,235	62,807
2001	-12%	$6,447,855	925,203	296,223	57,095
2002	-22%	$5,024,437	722,291	232,316	46,035
2003	29%	$6,459,474	930,787	301,119	61,730
2004	11%	$7,164,483	1,034,274	336,099	70,664
2005	5%	$7,512,677	1,084,540	352,433	74,098
2006	15%	$8,694,884	1,259,259	412,409	90,450
2007	5%	$9,163,538	1,327,133	434,638	95,325
2008	-39%	$5,601,431	813,388	268,074	60,754
2009	27%	$7,116,358	952,155	342,993	79,699
2010	15%	$8,186,112	1,097,278	396,742	93,954
2011	2%	$8,347,378	1,118,894	404,558	95,805
2012	16%	$9,666,264	1,295,679	468,478	110,942
2013	32%	$12,759,468	1,710,296	618,390	146,443
Avg.	12%	12%	11%	13%	11%

Ibbotson Associates **Stocks average 11.4% per year, bonds 5%, CDs 3%.** Stocks have gone up as much as 54% and as low as –43% in 1 year, up to 28% or down to –12% in 5 years, up 20% or down 0% in 10 years, up 18% or up 3% in 20 years. Short term bonds have gone up 14% or up 0% in 1 year, up 11% or up 0% in 5 years, up 9% or up 0% in 10 years, up 10% or up 1% in 20 years.

No money manager

"In every single time period and data point tested, low-cost funds beat high-cost funds."

According to an unbiased Morningstar study, low-cost funds beat high-cost funds PERIOD. However, the myth of Wall Street is that you must pay more for good performance. Not true—Buffett just proved it again, winning $1 million bet from 'professionals'. We all know that for most groceries' prices, paying more (for packaging and TV commercials) does not guarantee the best product. Warren Buffett's mentor, Benjamin Graham, advised: "buy financial products like we buy "groceries, … not perfume."

The BEST predictor of your investing and wealth building success is **low cost**. It is common sense that there are just too many variables in the success of growing companies' stocks for anyone to be able to pick them in advance on a consistent basis. A low-cost stock mutual fund provides the best chance of maximizing our accumulations as the market leaders change *over time*.

Contrary to Wall Street's hype, it does not matter which stocks are rising or falling at any given time. If our account holds a broad representation of stocks and our investment costs are low, we will benefit over the long haul. We own them all!

This is the smart strategy. When we subtract the costs of buying and maintaining investments, we give up a lot of the gains. We can use an online compounding calculator to become familiar with total accumulations at different rates of return—3, 5, 7, 9, 11: moneychimp.com/calculator/compound_interest_calculator.htm

Since the annual returns of stock funds have averaged 10-12% over time, we want to pick the lowest cost mutual fund available. A stock fund that reflects the overall market is called an index fund. This kind of fund costs only 0.04% ($4 per $10,000). Our account will compound at or near the 10-12% over time since the costs are low compared to ones that charge 1-3%. If we use the high-cost stock funds in our account, we will earn 7-8.5% over time. These funds pay managers high salaries with expensive bonuses. The fund owners and sales staff are paid well also. This is the cash cow of Wall Street. You pay for them.

The chart below makes it clear. Over time, the costs we pay each year will cut our total accumulation by a THIRD or more. Instead of compounding at 10-12% annually on average, some people give up 1.5-3% of the earnings on their money to the middle person. They end up with less.

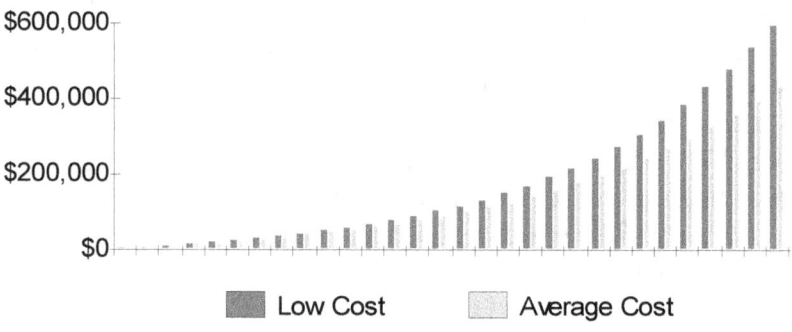

Wall Street says that we can earn more by paying a star manager to pick the right stocks on an ongoing basis. The money "experts" say we get what we pay for and a proven stock-picking manager will overcome the extra costs and make more for us.

The problem is that this myth has been proven wrong. The lowest cost funds don't pay a star manager and owner big bucks but come out ahead over time. There are simply too many variables for anyone or computer program to pick the winning stocks all the time. Some of the lowest cost funds are called index funds. When we buy an index, we are buying a piece of many companies that reflect the market. This gives us the same annual returns as the overall market over time. We pay tiny expenses.

Many studies have proven that index funds beat funds run by stock pickers most of the time. Low-cost index funds beat 95% of funds with a stock-picking manager.
https://www.marketwatch.com/story/why-way-fewer-actively-managed-funds-beat-the-sp-than-we-thought-2017-04-24

When we investigate the experiences of the best money managers and advisors in the world, we find they recommend index funds to most people who invest as silent partners. Here are their statements:

Warren Buffett is probably history's greatest investor, in terms of results with $80 BILLION ($80 thousand million dollars) so far. He buys *companies* that provide valuable services to a great number of people. His company owns parts of Coke, GEICO, Fruit of the Loom, Benjamin Moore, Heinz, Burlington Northern, etc. http://www.berkshirehathaway.com/subs/sublinks.html
      He told Reuters: "A very low-cost index is going to beat a majority of the amateur-managed money or professionally-managed money."

Compare the odds of selecting the correct mutual fund. A fund's chance of beating the market in EACH year is 3 out of 100. nytimes.com/2009/02/22/your-money/stocks-and-bonds/22stra.html

Peter Lynch, brilliant manager, Magellan Fund "…you'd be just as well off if you'd invested in the S&P 500." *One Up on Wall Street*, 1989, p. 240.

Jonathan Clements, formerly ***The Wall Street Journal***
"Most people can do it themselves. ... By indexing, you don't just ensure that you will do better than most other investors. You will also enjoy the advantage of 'relative certainty.' . . . For most investors, Vanguard will be the place to go." *You've Lost It, Now What? How to beat the bear market and still retire on time*, 2003, p. 62, 70.

Charles D. Ellis, advisor to money managers
"The premise . . . that professional investment managers *can* beat the market . . . appears to be false. It is a loser's game. ... clients would have done better in a market fund." Returns are "splendidly predictable—on average and over time." *Investment Policy, How to Win the Loser's Game*, 1985, p. 5, 20, 34.

Jane Bryant Quinn, consumer advisor
"I'm a longtime booster of index mutual funds. These funds follow the market as a whole. Tons of research has shown that most money managers don't beat the markets they invest in, after costs.

Maybe your own stocks or funds have excelled in the past couple of years. But in most cases, you've also been taking extra risk. The odds of superior performance are against you, in the long run. Indexing puts the odds on your side." *Los Angeles Business Journal*, May 8, 2000

Charles Schwab founder, discount broker
"I put my money where my mouth is: most of the mutual fund investments I have are in index funds, approximately 75%. My core investments are index funds. Experienced investors have discovered that in any given year, on average, only 20 to 30 percent of mutual funds outperform the market. That is why I recommend index funds…"
Mr. Schwab tells of one of his friends who owned many well-run funds. After keeping track of all the dividends, taxes, reinvestments tax basis and statements, he found he earned the same return as the index of these funds. After selling them all, he bought the index fund. He has "what he wanted in the first place: diversification, tax advantages, one statement, and lower expenses." *Guide to Financial Independence*, 1998, pp. 90, 103, 111.

Motley Fool, Internet site about investing
"Almost **everything** that you will ever read about mutual funds beyond, "Buy an index fund." is superfluous to your long-term success in investing in mutual funds." Fool.com.

Walter Updegrave, senior editor, *Money*
"Mutual fund picking would be easier if there was one you could count on to outperform 70% or so of its competitors over long stretches of a decade or more. It's called an index fund. Although less than 10% of investors own an index fund, they are "one of the best-kept secrets" on Wall Street. My unabashed aim is to convince you to put at least a part of your money into one or more of these funds. You have a far less than 50% chance of beating the market…. I strongly recommend that you make index funds your primary holding…." *The Right Way to Invest in Mutual Funds*, 1996, p 189-194.

Andrew Tobias, financial writer
"Scrimp and save, putting whatever you can into no-load, low-

expense stock market <u>index funds,</u> both U.S. and foreign. You will do better than 80% of your friends and neighbors." *My Vast Fortune*, 1997, p. 158.

There are many books written on the subject of index and "managed" funds. If you wish to vanquish the hype and understand investing, skim *A Random Walk Down Wall Street* by Princeton University's Burton Malkiel. Here are the reasons why smart insiders use low-cost funds:

1. Both stock and bond index funds provide better returns than 95% of managed funds for periods greater than 15 years.
2. You earn more because you pay less and no taxes.
3. Low-cost funds build greater wealth over time.
4. Low-cost funds can be less volatile because they reflect whole sectors of the market.
5. Low-cost funds offer better diversification.
6. You know what you are paying for. No high-salary managers.
7. Low-cost funds don't require you to hope the manager will predict the future correctly. The odds of doing it are 1 in 15,000 each year separately. Over time, all funds provide average returns minus their costs.
8. Low-cost funds are easy to buy.

> "Professional money management is a gigantic rip-off."
> Bill Gross, star bond manager, *Everything You've Heard About Investing is Wrong*

Summary of many studies about investing

First, fund managers try to predict the future of the market when they buy and sell securities in their funds. There is no <u>proof</u> this can be done well over time. <u>Yesterday's winners are usually tomorrow's losers.</u> The AVERAGE market return has been 10-12%, so a few managers will beat the average by luck—Just not the same ones every year. nytimes.com/2008/07/13/business/13stra.html
Second, the costs of the manager, their staff and operations <u>must be paid for by you</u> whether or not they earn you a dime. It is always better to pay as little as possible for the same benefits.

Costs can take 63% of your returns over time. Surprisingly, while the stock index rose 11%, investors with high paid managers averaged only **3.79%** annually from 1983-2013 (QAIB). DALBARinc.com.

Third, high cost managers get paid for increasing the size of their funds, not for making you rich. Bringing in more money is a full-time job. It is expensive to market the funds given that there are now thousands available. It is inevitable that popular funds will grow until they produce average returns with high expenses. Managers want to be rich, not right. online.wsj.com/article/SB10001424127887324059704578471154109438438.html

Fourth, there is much less chance of you being treated poorly by fund management if the structure and governance are customer-oriented like Vanguard's and TIAA's are.

Fifth, many professional managers and Wall Street insiders place their core assets in low-cost index funds. https://www.marketwatch.com/story/why-wall-street-hates-our-lazy-portfolios-strategy-1332871750552

The best predictor of the success of a mutual fund is its **cost**. Usually the least expensive funds that match market averages beat the more expensive managed funds. Low-cost market index funds buy all the securities represented in a broad market. The goal of an index fund is to match its market. Low-cost index funds have provided returns that beat 83-95% of managed funds over the long-term. No Wall Street guru has been able to predict the future. The returns regress to the mean of 10-12%. The smart money is on the averages not the long shot. We maximize the *Miracle of Compounding* by buying and holding low-cost investments.

"In every single time period and data point tested, low-cost funds beat high-cost funds."

Mutual funds

If we want to have a $1,000,000 tax-FREE account, we need a way to make it happen—a strategy. We need to know how and where to invest, invest regularly, invest properly, monitor accumulations along the way, and get help when we need it. We need a clear plan that takes only one hour to set up and only one hour per year to manage. Complicated plans just don't work for most people. Complicated strategies cost more to execute.

Picking *individual* stocks as a strategy is not likely to work for us. Professional managers and day traders have had limited success over time. Our strategy is to build wealth as a silent partner in growing global companies. Since it is unlikely that we (or anyone else) will be able to pick the next Google or Apple, we invest in a large group of firms. We do not need to fear picking the wrong one or picking one at the wrong time. As the founder of the largest mutual fund firm, John Bogle, says: "Don't look for the needle. Buy the haystack." This is a proven successful strategy.

Of course, this is contrary to the myth of Wall Street 'professional' gurus. We make our living claiming to find the needle every year and you pay us dearly year after year. We promise that the magical stock pickers can find the next big one and you pay us well because you want to be rich.

Like the lottery, we kid ourselves into thinking that "someone has to win, why not me." We don't believe we are wasting our money even though our rational mind knows that our chance of winning is very low. Managed funds don't beat the market most of the time. The odds are like those of a lottery—18 million to 1. Like the lottery, when we invest in a managed fund to "beat the market" we don't count up the costs of the "tickets." We may buy $25 worth of tickets a week and end up winning $1,000 in a year. We spent $1,200 for $1,000.

In the same manner, a mutual fund manager advertises that their fund has "beaten" the market and so we pay 1.5-3% of our assets every year. Over time we find that while the stock market index rose 10.38% from 1990-2010, we earned only **2.56%** annually. This is what happened to retail investors according to Dalbar's QAIB recent study. DALBARinc.com

Many retail investors keep switching to the hot funds or stocks according to the advertising we run regularly. Some are always chasing the last most successful story. Some buy at the high point because they want the winner. They sell when it falls and they want the next high flier. Over time they never earn the return promised by our managers.

In this way, costs can take 40% of their returns over time. Each time they sell and buy, they give up earnings and perhaps part of their money if they use a sales person charging 5%. Even if they stay with one managed mutual fund that has annual fees of 1.5-3%, they are killing the miracle of compounding.

Using the compounding calculator, we can see that our accumulation drops to $0.6 million if we earn 9% instead of 11% annually. We could have $2 million in 40 years at 11%. moneychimp.com/calculator/compound_interest_calculator.htm

Another Wall Street myth is that investing in market index funds will produce average (mediocre) returns. It is true that the returns will be close to the returns of the market. However, historically the market returns are the ones that are somewhat predictable and not bad. Investing in growing companies provides no guaranteed return but the average returns have held steady since the 1930s when they started keeping records.

Wall Street history is littered with strategies that were said to beat the market. The brilliant stock pickers have also come and gone. Today, though, which one of the new ones are you going to invest with? No one knows. The ONLY thing we really know is that the averages of broad market indexes have produced 10-12% on average over time.

For example, some of our clients use these Vanguard mutual funds which have earned over 11% for a long time. Of course, there is no guarantee of future returns, but they have all done fairly well. Most started with the 500 Index and added companies in the Energy, Health and International sectors. These 10 funds have done well over time. Many investors pick Vanguard funds because the funds are well run at cost. No "bells and whistles." No expensive managers and overhead. No owner taking profits from the investment returns.

2013 Total Return	Fund	Long-term Return*	Longevity
32.3%	500 Index	11.0%*	since 1976
18.4%	Energy	13.2%	since 1984
38.4%	Extended Market	11.2%	since 1987
43.2%	Health	17.1%	since 1984
23.0%	International Growth	11.2%	since 1981
39.7%	PRIMECAP	13.7%	since 1984
37.6%	Small Cap Index	10.9%	since 1960
9.2%	Wellesley Income	10.1%	since 1970
36.1%	Windsor	11.6%	since 1958
30.7%	Windsor II	11.1%	since 1985
30.9%	Average	12.1%	

*Average Annual Returns as of 12/31/13.

These investors are long-term investors, not speculators. They believe that investments in low-cost funds (index and managed) are their best chance of reaching their goals. They have been rewarded for that belief. Vanguard has many low-cost funds and their service is better than most funds. I own some of them.

Remember, we are investing for the long-term. Most pension funds are invested in stock and bond indexes. Even though the market fell 22% in 2002 and jumped 29% in 2003, the average was still holding. Average returns mean we do not suffer the lowest lows nor the highest highs. They regress to the mean: 10-12%.

Most of the largest growing companies in the world are held by these funds. Large US firms are now earning at least half of their profits overseas so we are benefiting from growth around the world. This is important because we don't want to miss important earnings progress as the developing nations like China and India expand their economies.

We don't know exactly which companies will be winners but we want to participate in all of them. We want to own some smaller growing companies too. If they become successful, they will move to the large company funds. We are exposed to almost all areas of the global economy by buying shares of these mutual funds at the lowest cost. We suffer the ups and downs of the markets just like every investor. However, we see that some funds do better at certain times while others do worse. Together we see clients hitting their goal of 10-12% average annual returns.

This type of investing has the greatest chance of avoiding severe swings in the balance of our accumulation. This type of strategy—investing in different types and sizes of companies in different sectors around the world—is called Modern Portfolio Theory.

Modern Portfolio Theory

Some clients use the MPT strategy to control risk while increasing returns. MPT (Moneychimp.com/articles/risk/riskintro.htm) holds that if we put our eggs in different baskets of assets that grow at different times, then the value of all our eggs grows with fewer ups and downs. We can manage the ups and downs of equity funds by buying different ones over time. Higher risk assets are small caps, REITs and foreign stocks. This strategy earns 10-12% with 30% less volatility.

Members assemble asset classes (see callan.com/research/download/?file=periodic/free/457.pdf) that fit their risk-reward tastes. According to this Nobel Prize-winning strategy moneychimp.com/articles/risk/portfolio.htm, a high return asset with a low correlation to other assets in the portfolio can actually reduce the volatility of the whole. It may be possible to earn high returns with less risk **overall** as each asset goes up and down at different times. See the example at fool.com/personal-finance/retirement/2007/03/06/5-steps-to-salvage-your-retirement.aspx.

The past provides only PROBABLE futures. But isn't $1,000,000 (plus or minus $100,000) better than $150,000. Your $250-per-month deposit in the bank for 33 years will be worth about $100,000 after tax compared with about $1 million from stock investing with no tax. Every investor would be better off with $1 million (+/- $100,000) than $150,000 from a bank.

When young investors begin investing, they cannot buy all 10 Vanguard funds at once with $250 per month. Vanguard has minimums on all funds so they can keep their expenses low for everyone.

There are two ways to start our Roth IRA account. The easiest way is to save $250 a month in our savings account until we have the $1,000 minimum for Vanguard's entry fund: STAR STAR #56. We can open the Roth IRA by phone or online: STAR minimum is $1,000. Most Vanguard funds need $3,000 to start. We can keep contributing to this index fund until we have $3,000 for the 500 Index and then $3,000 for the Extended Market funds. Vanguard is at 877-662-7447.

The second way to begin is to open a Roth IRA at TIAA, the world's largest pension company, primarily for educational and research institutions. Low expenses and low initial contributions make TIAA an organization we can stay with for life. TIAA 800.842.2888.

At TIAA.org, we can make application and begin immediately with an automatic monthly contribution of $100 or more from our bank account. We can follow how the assets grow by themselves. TIAA has two funds that provide us with the diversity of companies worldwide: TIAA Equity Index and TIAA International Equity.

Request a prospectus (owner's manual) for each fund you will be using at Vanguard or TIAA. Both mutual fund firms have experienced salaried representatives that provide accurate information about accounts and funds. Both offer low-cost index funds that hold a broad representation of the market returns of 10-12%. This is a building block to accumulating wealth.

Both firms are focused on you, not on profits.

This strategy is to buy stocks of growing companies worldwide. No Wall Street guru can predict the future winners. Most can't do better than 50%—a flip of the coin. Your investments provide long-term growth of 10-12% annually on average with the benefit of avoiding single company or industry failures. It provides exposure to new growth potential around the world with less risk than holding one company, one sector, or one country. Some years our account is up 33% and some years down 22%. However, we double our money every 7-9 years *over time.*

It is the amount we KEEP that matters!

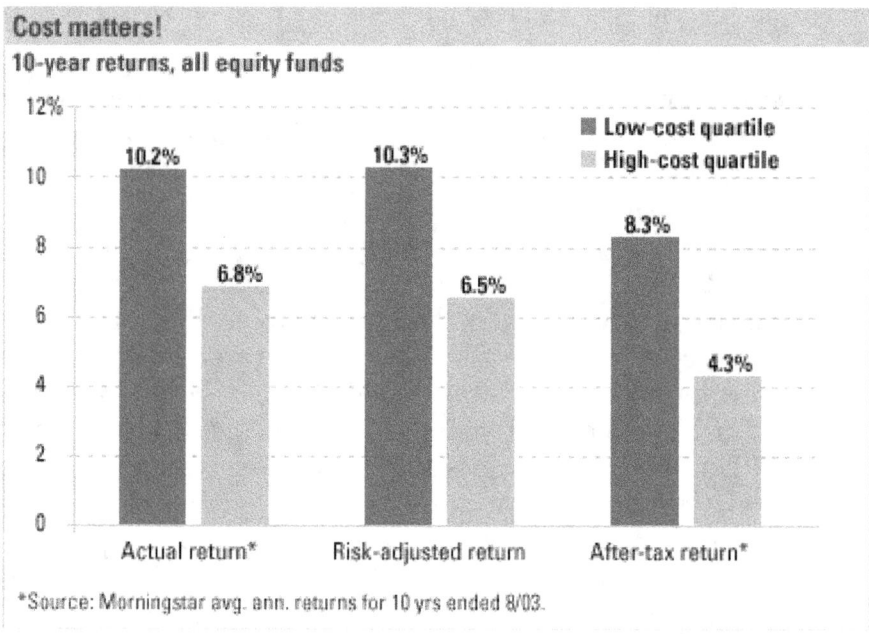

Automatic Investing

We need to find at least $250 per month to invest in order to build our account. We can build wealth by following the strategy outlined in the previous chapters, but we need to have at least $250 available in the first place. In my experience, it doesn't matter how much people earn, most say they don't have the money to invest for their future. "Today is hard enough," they complain.

Yes, that may well be, but if we don't find the $250 we won't have a very happy tomorrow. We have to go back to our goal. We want to build wealth: accumulating $1,000,000 over time. Based on the way wealth compounds, we need to identify at least $250 a month on a permanent basis. We need to be consistent for the **miracle of compounding** to work.

Budget is a dirty word so we won't use it. No one wants to be restricted in their spending. Even the people who know they are wasting $100 a month on the lottery, still play. I know it satisfies an immediate riches fantasy. However, people change when they see the **power of compounding** in their account.

I want to explain how you can find at least $250 a month to invest from a different perspective. If we are going to spend all of our income, we need to adopt a "spending plan" with the $250 a month for investment included in it. Otherwise, we won't accumulate $1,000,000. Even if we don't have 33 years, our $250 could grow to a significant sum.

A Spending Plan is a way to set priorities for our regular spending. We can accumulate $1 million to accomplish all that we want to do in life by using just 10 percent of our income to buy assets that "grow by themselves." We invest $250 a month for 33 years—just $99,000—and time makes it $1,000,000. $3,000 a year just happens to be the amount of the average tax refund. So you may have found the $250 a month you need for $1 million fund.

Using a Spending Plan is **like brushing your teeth**—it's a habit that isn't that difficult to learn—then it is automatic. If we want our plan to become a habit, we have to practice it. If we consciously spend our income on those items on our priority list, we can't fail to develop the habit. We are teaching ourselves that we can have whatever we want in time. We are not saying "no" to that desire. We are saying put it on our list. We will get what we want eventually.

First, our Spending Plan must include what we need to function. Our future is part of our immediate needs in the sense that if we don't prepare now, we won't have the future we want. Again, building a $1,000,000 account is a lifelong process and requires making a commitment. Like building a business, it takes planning and following the steps we talked about so far.

There are a number of ways to identify the $250 a month we need to build our future. Some investors include the $250 in their automatic bill payment or have the trustee debit their account automatically. The contribution is just another bill like rent, mortgage, utilities, car payment, cable, phone, etc. They live on the balance of their income.

Others set up family goals and decide to put a certain amount in a separate account for each goal. In this way, they keep the wealth building process in the forefront of their monthly bill payments ritual.

Whatever way works for you. The important thing is to change the status of wealth building from a vague future desire to a monthly habit. "Set it up and forget it" is the theme of investing.

Most people find that the easiest way is to set up an automatic debit of their checking account by the trustee at the time of the application for the Roth IRA. If we are using a Roth 401k or other employer account, we set up the retirement account with automatic contributions. We can have an IRA and our 401k at work but if there is no employer match, the Roth IRA is better—it's tax-FREE.

The Spending Plan works for all types of goals: college fund, emergency fund, vacation fund, new used car fund, business start-up fund, whatever we decide to put at the top of our list of priorities. If we don't have this list, we can make one easily.

Clients who are successful have made written plans in some form or other. They have some idea of how much they will need at some time in the future. For short-term goals we can use our savings account but for long-term goals we need to use higher return securities. Many clients have trouble deciding which investment to use for each goal.

I explain the chart we displayed on page 6 above. Stock mutual funds are the investment of choice for any long-term accumulation goal. As per the chart, annual returns of 10-12% are the norm for any accumulation over 10-15 years. Once we have $150,000 in a long-term account, we can "borrow" from ourselves for short-term needs as long as keep buying 'assets that grow by themselves.'

Thus, clients have used their long-term accumulation account for vacations, cars, appliances, emergencies, etc. This works if they keep contributing. The account is set up as a Roth IRA so the *contributions* are not taxed when used before age 59.5. After that age, there are no taxes at all—NEVER. However, to meet our long-term goals, we have to add a little more each month to let our money keep working for us. Every $1,000 is worth $50,000 later.

Another benefit of using a Spending Plan is that we become focused on how we spend our money. We are more inclined to buy only what we need. For most of us, when we go grocery shopping, we seek to get the most for our money by shopping for discounts and by buying in bulk. In the last ten years, the financial services industry has started to offer better values on products. We can avoid overpaying Wall Street firms and avoid buying products we really don't need.

How do we know? ***The Insiders Guides*** I compiled with colleagues provides an easy way to save $3,000 or more on financial products we already use. There are buyer's guides for each specific area. We review some of the ways to find $250 a month in savings in the next chapter.

We can't build wealth by spending more than we earn. Building wealth takes patience and commitment to contributing to our investment business every month. Some people don't try to be disciplined investors. They let the trustee debit the $250 or 10% every month so they can't fail to become a millionaire.

Time is the crucial factor in building wealth because of the ***miracle of compounding***. Only automatic investing guarantees you are sticking with your Spending Plan.

Are you paying too much?

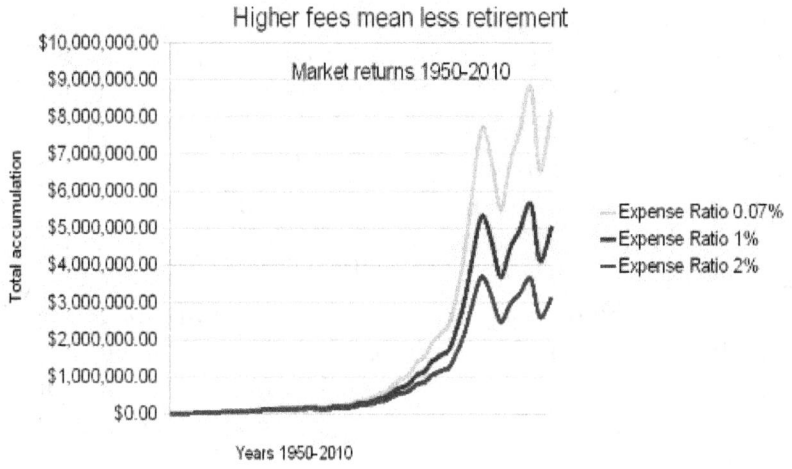

Low-cost beats high-cost

It is easy to build wealth if we already have a pile of money. It takes 7-9 years to accumulate $1 million if you already have $500,000. Check the chart.

Monthly	Accumulation at 12% per year									
	5	10	15	20	25	30	35	40	45	50
$100	$8,167	$23,004	$49,958	$98,925	$187,884	$349,496	$643,095	$1,176,477	$2,145,469	$3,905,834
$200	$16,334	$46,008	$99,916	$197,850	$375,768	$698,992	$1,286,190	$2,352,954	$4,290,938	$7,811,668
$300	$24,501	$69,012	$149,874	$296,775	$563,652	$1,048,488	$1,929,285	$3,529,431	$6,436,408	$11,717,502
$500	$40,835	$115,020	$249,790	$494,625	$939,420	$1,747,480	$3,215,475	$5,882,385	$10,727,346	$19,529,169

But how do we capture that first $500,000, that $250,000, or even that first $50,000? It comes from buying assets that 'grow by themselves.' It takes time and the easiest way to make sure we reach our goal is to make our monthly contributions automatic.

But where do we get the $250 a month? The best way is to "REDIRECT" the **cash we already spend** on things we really don't need or can buy for less.

I think most working people waste $3,000 or more each year on financial services. They can stop paying for services they don't need. This takes the same type of questioning we go through when buying any commodity. When we buy groceries, do we buy the house brand or the one on sale or the one we see advertised?

In buying insurance or mutual funds, do we do research, compare costs and buy value? Do we pay an extra $1000 to buy the one the sales person is highlighting? The difference between paying full price for a new car and a 3-year-old model can be 40% or more. When we put our future on top of our priority list, we can REDIRECT the savings to a more worthwhile purpose. This is how millionaires become and *stay* millionaires.

It is the same with financial services. Most of us are not used to shopping for insurance, mutual funds, banking and mortgages. So we don't. We are operating under the mythology of Wall Street —'professionals' say we need them to help guide us, for a price.

But you don't need us anymore. The world has changed.

Let's take some examples of **annual savings**:

Auto insurance: save $400 or more EVERY year by changing/dropping some benefits we don't need.

Home insurance: save $200 or more EVERY year by changing one limit.

Life insurance: save $1,000 or more EVERY year by using direct to consumer insurer.

Mutual funds: save $2-3,000 EVERY year by using low-cost providers.

Bank: save $120 EVERY year by using a low-cost provider of the benefits we usually use.

Mortgage: save $2,000 on closings and lower interest rates.

Investments: earn 15-30% guaranteed just by paying off credit cards.

Tax refund: Averages $3,022 and usually spent.

Using the Insiders' Guides I put together in the book ***The Insiders' Guides to Buying Discount Financial Services: Buy Direct and Save $3,000 Every Year,*** we can REDIRECT the $250 a month without having to give up anything important. We don't need to tighten our belt or make a budget. We can give up things we would not benefit from anyway.

I offer a number of testimonials from people who have told me about their experience using the ***Guides***.

George B. New York:
"I saved $1,356 on my vehicle insurance using your Insider's Guide to Vehicle Insurance. I saved by using some of your Insiders' 'tricks of the trade' like dropping the extras that I already had."

John D. New York:
"I canceled my life insurance and used the money to buy the mutual funds. You were right. I didn't need the insurance anymore. My kids are all grown. My new wife and I invest as much as we can now. Your Guide to 'Living' Insurance is a great way to look at our insurance needs."

Mark K. Ohio:
"I had no idea how to invest in the 401k that my new job offered. I have not been disappointed with the mutual funds suggested by

other members. I saved about a $1,000 by transferring my old 401k mutual funds to the low-cost funds in your Guide. When I sold my primary residence in 2004, I followed members' advice with the gains. I use all your Guides to help me save more for my retirement since I got a late start. Thanks."

I have a great example of the big savings we can expect by shopping for insurance. I found that people usually pick name brands instead of shopping for services they need. Companies spend a lot for TV advertising and gimmicks.

Example:

MetLife charged $983 for a $300,000 30-year **term policy**. This same $300,000 benefit was sold by Savings Bank Life Insurance for $384 a year. Their financial strength ratings are A+ and their underwriting requirements are the same. The difference, $599, over 30 years is $17,970. If invested, this difference can add $175,000 to OUR **account**.

Most people are amazed at the difference a little research and shopping can accomplish. Even if we did not have the *Guide*, a search of the Internet would reveal several portals that quote rates. Unfortunately, most people don't take the time to shop or don't know exactly what they need. The *Guides* help us make the decision of where to shop and what to buy.

Buy financial products like you buy "groceries not perfume" is the advice of value investor Benjamin Graham. Buying only what we need in every financial service area will provide the cash for contributions. **We give up nothing and gain our future**. Taking the time to shop in each area of our expenses helps us make our future happen. Shopping for an hour can add $175,000 to our account over time.

Yes, it is worth it! You pay less and get more.

This strategy—to cut out the middle people who are taking your money with little benefit to you—makes sense and works!

Consistency means you end up with 11%

2011 Total Return	Fund	Long-term Return*	Longevity
1.97%	500 Index	10.36%	since 1976
-1.74%	Energy	12.71%	since 1984
-3.73%	Extended Market	9.96%	since 1987
11.45%	Health	16.30%	since 1984
-13.68%	International Growth	10.50%	since 1981
-1.84%	PRIMECAP	12.79%	since 1984
-2.80%	Small Cap Index	10.26%	since 1960
9.63%	Wellesley Income	10.16%	since 1970
-4.00%	Windsor	11.00%	since 1958
2.70%	Windsor II	10.18%	since 1985
0.00%	Average	11.42%	

*Average Annual Returns as of 12/31/11.

Don't *look* twice—it's alright

> "We continue to make more money when *snoring* than when active."
> Warren Buffett, Berkshirehathaway.com/

This is the advice of the most successful investor of our day. He is making it clear that we should NOT touch our investments very often. Contrary to the advice of the Wall Street 'professionals,' he leaves his assets alone to compound over time. He does not follow the 'hot' investment of the day. He buys the stocks of growing companies. He has held some investments for over 40 years.

Our emotions tell us to sell when our account balance goes down as it did in 2011. We want to buy the next big investment to make up for previous losses. This is why we have a hard time following Buffett's advice. However, the emotions that cause us to be bad investors are what we can control—not the stock price of growing companies worldwide.

Our contributions to our **account** need to be automatic so we buy more *shares* when the market is down and less when it is up. This helps us control our emotions. When the market is down, we need to look at the line graph on page 13. We don't know when the market will be up or down but we see that if we sell, we may miss the next advance. This is why we have to remember Warren Buffett's advice and hold on to stocks/stock funds. In fact, Mr Buffett says **"our favorite holding period is forever."** http://www.berkshirehathaway.com/letters/1988.html

When we own a broad cross-section of the market, we really don't have to worry about buying and selling our investments. There is no better investment for the long term. Besides, what would we buy if we sold? Bank CD at 1-2%? We have seen that stocks are the safest investment for periods over 10 years.

From my experience, there is only one way to avoid bad investment decisions: Do NOT make any investment decisions in haste. Stick with the idea that we only have to look at our tax-FREE account once a year. At that time, I make sure I am making contributions to the specific mutual fund I need to build in order to keep them equally balanced. That is the simplest way.

For instance, when I first started investing, I used the 500 Index. After I had accumulated enough to buy the Extended Market, I sold shares of the 500 Index ($3,000) and bought it. I kept investing into the 500 Index until I had the minimum for the next one on the list. I repeated this pattern until I had the minimum in each. Then I picked one to add $250 a month for one year. The next year, I did the same until I completed the list again and again.

Today, I am still making contributions using the same rotation because I still have earned income. My wife does too. Once a year, I compare the account balances. I note what happened during the year for any one fund. I go to the Vanguard site and <u>read about that fund</u>. Do I need to make a change? No, usually I don't. I use the 10 funds listed above. They have done well consistently over the years. I buy more shares every month automatically.

Notice that when we buy each fund at first, we have to sell shares in the 500 Index to do so. Because we are using a Roth IRA, there is no tax on this sale if the share price has gone up. Also, each year, our dividends are re-invested without paying tax on that income. This is part of the **miracle of compounding**. Our account is growing without taxes each year. Any other non-retirement account would be diminished by the tax and fee paid each year.

There is no need to sell funds that have done well in order to re-balance the 10 funds' balances equally. Most of the research shows that re-balancing each year does not change the long-term outcome of the whole portfolio. Some clients use their contributions each year to add to the fund that has grown the *least*. However, as each fund becomes larger, the effect of adding contributions becomes smaller over time.

When we have to sell shares to meet an emergency or avoid interest payments by using cash for large ticket items, we may sell shares in each fund by equal dollar amounts. This is a better strategy than selling shares in only one fund since we don't know which fund may recover the fastest going forward. In the same way as accumulating shares, we need to reimburse our accounts for the amounts used. We can contribute up to $5,500 a year. It is very desirable to also continue to make contributions. This way we are assured of catching up to our position as we reach our goal.

However, we found that after accumulating a large proportion of our goal, adding the $250 per month did not seem to matter to the outcome. For instance, our client whose account is shown on page 22 took $25,000 for a used luxury car in the year the account hit over half a million. He also stopped making contributions. His account total did not suffer long term.

Actually this client redirected his $250 monthly contribution to his grandchild's Roth IRA **account** so that they might have a financial foundation all their life. If he keeps giving this $3,000 a year to his offspring for 40 years, they could have $2,000,000 by age 50. The grandchild "earns" $3,000 a year doing odd jobs for him. Learn more about this "Gift of a Lifetime" in my book, amazon.com/Give-your-Grandchild-000-Lifetime/.

Manage investments once a year is wise advice. Our tax-FREE account does not require us to hire an advisor to manage it. Advisors do not know what the future holds anymore than we do so paying them 1-3% each year just reduces our annual returns. Their fees/charges can take up to 63% of our total accumulations over time. Index funds beat managed funds 83-95% of the time!

We are investing for the long term and there is no proof that switching from one fund or stock to another during the year does anything to help our results. As we add more contributions, we can rotate through each fund we use. The less we tamper with our account the better.

The *Miracle of Compounding* only works when we do NOT let 'professionals' manage our money. Buffett has said that many give their money and fees to managers because they think they and their managers are smarter than the market.

Hubris kills their future.

Your Action Plan

This week:
Goal

This month:
Goal

This year:
Goals

Spend wisely—it's your future

My wife and I have used the 10 funds to build wealth. We have learned to be patient and accumulate enough for the future. We have paid back any amounts that we borrowed to pay cash for large purchases. We have been fortunate that the historical averages of market returns have produced the accumulations we wished.
    NOW WHAT?
Now we take about 8% out of the account each year and pay no income taxes on the Roth portion. As of 2018, most states follow the IRS code on our **account**, a Roth IRA—§ 408 trust account. https://www.irs.gov/pub/irs-pdf/p590b.pdf
    Some clients have moved some of their accumulations into a balanced fund like Wellesley Income in order to provide a monthly check to their checking account for their regular expenses. They created a retirement spending plan that assured them of that monthly income of a fixed dollar amount with this ***Guide***. amazon.com/Your-Retirement-Spending-Plan-enough
    We have to create our $1,000,000 nest egg in order to provide the same buying power as we have today because of inflation. I am assuming that most working families will need at least $50,000 a year to live on in retirement. We don't know what will happen to Social Security by 2034. We don't know what employer pensions might look like by then. I am assuming that inflation will continue at a 3% rate. It might be more or less. I have no idea. However, we must prepare for inflation. Planning is crucial to success.
    At 3%, inflation will make the goods we buy now for $50,000 cost about $80,000. This is not exact. I don't know what will happen in 40 days let alone 40 years. If Social Security or employer pensions can add to our basic income, that is fine. But we don't want to count on them.
    I am using $50,000 as a basic-needs income because that has been my experience of what working people desire. It is also an amount that could be generated by our $1,000,000 account balance. Many clients use 6-8% as a target for their investment returns in retirement. This is just an approximation of the average returns

over time. In lean years, they take out less.

Some clients move half their balances into a bond or balanced fund in order to generate the income for the coming year. The balance of their account remains in the broad stock funds we have listed above. These funds will continue to produce returns in the 10-12% range. If there is a bad year like 2008, we are not taking money out of our principal at a bad time. We take the money from a bond fund like the Vanguard Total Bond which has traditionally been less volatile.

The funds we have listed above include some of the most consistent low volatility returns over time. The <u>Wellesley Income</u> fund has produced almost 10% per year on average since 1970. It contains stocks and bonds. **This fund alone might be our source** of annual withdrawals of principal and dividends. Since our Roth account is not taxable, there are no tax considerations in the decision of which fund to tap for our monthly income.

Because we have no tax liability on this income of $80,000 per year, we may not have to pay tax on our other income like Social Security and/or our qualified retirement funds. 85% of Social Security benefits are currently subject to federal income taxes. The IRS <u>worksheet</u> determines the percentage based on all our other income. Typically those with little or no other income currently have no tax due on their Social Security benefits. Pensions are taxed as income since we did not pay tax on the contributions.

In most cases, we will pay little income tax on our income in retirement since the bulk of it, $80,000 ($50,000 adjusted for inflation), will be tax-FREE. This will give us up to 30% more cash to spend compared with others who do not have this account. Pensions and other taxable income may be taxed at even higher rates in the future to pay for the two wars and three tax cuts that we endured since 2001. We have never gone to war and taken tax breaks at the same time before so this will take time to work out.

Our tax-FREE income will provide us with our basic-needs income and if we continue to follow the same 10 steps of building wealth, we will find a comfortable lifestyle throughout the 30 to 40 years of not working unless we want to.

I and many clients are assuming we will work at least part time after we take full retirement and begin collecting Social Security. If benefits are cut, we will need to work. We are encouraged to use our tax-FREE income to develop a small business since this can help us control the income that is taxed.

As I mentioned at the beginning of this book, many working millionaires are self-employed. Running a small business is a great way to control the taxes they pay. Taxes are the biggest killer of wealth building that exists. It destroys the compounding factor.

The accumulation of $1,000,000 over time can be achieved with patience and perseverance. Spending the income that $1,000,000 can generate may require us to take some principal from time to time. If we use the same 10 steps of wealth building to do this, we will probably have enough to take care of long-term health care and other unforeseen expenses. Since we don't know what may happen, we will want to continue the same habits we have developed before retirement. We live within our means.

We may find that we will have a sizable legacy as we age. There are many ways to pass on our wealth that don't require an attorney on contingency or complicated legal formulations. Many clients have found that incremental gifts to charity and family provide immediate gratification. They have used the suggestions for wealth transfer I presented in the ***Retirement Spending Plan***.

Plan purchases and retirement spending wisely. Planning assures that our retirement income is tax-FREE and has the purchasing power of about $50,000 in today's dollars. Working millionaires typically don't go out and buy a mansion and the trappings of the wealthy when they retire. They usually have paid off their homes. They travel and share with family. Some continue to earn income doing what they enjoy or provide help to others in their volunteer efforts.

This is your life when you become a ***tax-FREE millionaire*** without Wall Street 'professionals' taking a bite out of your retirement income.

Remember, it is ***compounding*** that beats stock picking.

The Keys to Wealth

1. **Costs matter**: Broker/advisor cost 1% to 3% every year

   If you use a salesperson, costs take HALF your money!
   $3,000 per year @11%   for 33 years = $1,018,177
   $3,000 per year @11-1% for 33 years = $778,768
   $3,000 per year @11-2% for 33 years = $613,805
   $3,000 per year @11-3% for 33 years = $486,634
   www.moneychimp.com/calculator/compound_interest_calculator.htm

2.   Broker/advisor stock-picking does not beat index funds over time. No money manager has been able to beat the markets consistently. No one can forecast the future. Buffett wins bet with index fund. https://www.cxoadvisory.com/gurus/

3. **Compounding** creates investment success; not buying AND selling. The chance of you doing both, at the right times, is near zero. Warren Buffett's holding period is "forever." No trading!

4. A **tax-FREE** investment account increases your balance 30%.

5. Putting all your money in one stock or market sector guarantees failure over time. No one investment is perfect. Buy a **group of growing global businesses.**

6. '**Dollar cost average**' buying technique lowers the cost of shares over time. When you invest a fixed amount each month, you buy more mutual fund shares when the price is low and less when high. Over time, you will own more shares at a lower average cost.

7. **Consistency** wins over the long term. Quick in and out trading only benefits Wall Street. Market timing may work for a short time but the odds of being right on the buy and sell are long.

8. **Patience** is required to allow your money to work for you. Building a business takes time. Investing is betting to most of us.

Buffett won and so can you

Most wealthy people have learned to use the strategies discussed above. That is why they stay rich. Sometimes they need to confirm the technical details. Now they do it for less and keep more. They don't use high-cost products or advisors. Some use the 10 Vanguard funds above. Many Wall Street owners, *not* sales people, use low-cost services.

Many clients have done research on their own and really just needed confirmation of their own thinking. They made the decisions but wanted to be sure there was nothing they were missing. The industry has made building wealth a mystery so that they could say, "you need us"—a "doctor" of financial health who you must pay very well. The industry takes $560 billions from investors' accounts year after year with limited improvement. Trading stocks usually does NOT benefit you. The average return was only 3.79%.

A person paying 1% to 3% of their portfolio every year to an advisor can't then admit they get very little for their money. 95% of advisors can't beat the investment returns of the market so that fee of $10,000 or more every year is really just a drag on income. Over time that fee compounds as your balance goes up and can take up to 63% of your total possible accumulations. Advisors like to buy and sell creating taxes and fees. But these costs hurt you.

As Buffett said, **compounding is key** to reaching our money goals. If we pay 2% to get 10-12%, we net 8-10%. Since we know that no advisor can guarantee 10-12% and most studies show investing directly without a 'professional' can yield the same result, there is no reason to give up 2%. Advisors usually charge 2% whether they beat the averages or not so it is better to go for the 10-12% on our own. **Advisors don't give refunds if they fail!**

The clear winning strategy is to use the 10 funds and let compounding work its magic. Over time using a tax-FREE account with low fees, we can accumulate $1,000,000 from $250 a month at 10-12%. Using a compounding calculator moneychimp.com/calculator/compound_interest_calculator.htm, we find the range is 31 to 35 years. If our spouse has an account, we can shorten the time to 26-29 years for a family $1 million.

If we use an advisor, we may give up over $500,000 of $1 million in total accumulation. Research has shown that the average investor actually earns about **3.79%** *not 11% annually* over time.

Our 10 funds for building wealth work because they are low-cost strategies inside a unique **tax-FREE trust account.** This eliminates the biggest killers of wealth: TAXES and FEES. We learned that compounding over time is the real engine for building wealth. Most people are NOT going to be successful at this because they have no patience to let compounding do the work.

We can be our own masters of tax-FREE wealth with patience. There is no need to pick stocks or hire expensive advisors or product pushers with hidden fees. We can do it ourselves as long as we have a plan. The plan is the following 10 steps:

1. Avoid taxes with a tax-advantaged trust account.
2. Use a lifetime investment plan.
3. Compound high earnings over time.
4. Make investing automatic.
5. Avoid high-cost investment products.
6. Buy assets that grow in any economy.
7. Invest at least 10% of income.
8. Buy financial products like you buy "groceries not perfume."
9. Manage investments once a year.
10. Plan purchases and retirement spending wisely.

You must take the first step. Advisors can't profit from these steps. You have to call Vanguard or TIAA *yourself* to set up your account. Advisors can't. It takes about an hour to set up a Roth IRA for both of you. You can do it online or by phone. You can begin with TIAA and $100 automatic contributions or Vanguard with $1,000. Put the contributions on automatic so you don't have to decide every month whether to invest. That is usually how people fail. Life happens and there is always an emergency that requires cash. But future life happens too and you want to be spending your $80,000 a year not praying Washington won't cut Social Security benefits every year.

If you have been investing, you can convert portions of your IRA each year, paying tax on the earnings as you go. Over time, your Roth account will grow with earnings that are tax-FREE. This money may reduce your overall taxes in retirement. It also is a great estate planning tool since no tax will be due from your heirs.

There is a clear reason why "working millionaires" become wealthy. It is not luck or inheritance. Millions of immigrants to this country have done it before. They lived below their means. They saved and invested in businesses. They did not let temporary cash flow problems stop them from building wealth. They used the same path to building wealth every day.

As many clients say, "I never even miss the contributions because I never see them. Then all of a sudden, I see my statement has $25,000, $50,000, $250,000, $1,000,000, $2,000,000. We are talking real money here."

The Miracle of Compounding
is the most important factor in building wealth.

My wife and I used and use this plan now. We have about $72,000 in retirement income. We have peace of mind that we will have enough no matter how long we need it. In fact, our **Wealth Reserve**™ keeps growing by itself.

Tax-advantaged wealth is a *habit* not a lottery.

Call Vanguard 800.551.8631 or TIAA 800.842.2888 today.

Just do it! Thank me later.

NOTES

The Author

Dan Keppel has been helping people find financial services that fit their lifestyles since working in a securities firm, an insurer, two banks and his own MoneyCoach service. His book, The Insiders' Guides to Buying Discount Financial Services: *Buy Direct and Save $3,000 Every Year,* shows you how, what and where to buy financial products like industry insiders do—directly from the highest rated companies for less. He edits TheInsidersGuides.com and was an adjunct at a local college. He lives in Montclair, NJ with his wife and two cats, Anu and Katze.

To receive Dan Keppel's weekly Alert of saving ideas, go to www.TheInsidersGuides.com or his blog at http://dankeppel.blogspot.com/

www.ingramcontent.com/pod-product-compliance
Lightning Source LLC
Chambersburg PA
CBHW030048230526
45471CB00003B/990